Seeing the Pandemic
with Eyes of Faith

CONTENTS

"Eyes" and "Backs"

For the first time, in 2020, the *Oxford English Dictionary* has found it impossible to name only one 'Word of the Year'. Too much has happened. More and more words seem to be needed to express our common lived experience: lockdown, transmission, social distancing, deep cleaning, pre-Covid and post-Covid, face mask, key workers, PPE, bubble, reopening… Has the Church any other words to add? I believe it has: the word "prophetic".

At the end of the sixth century the city of Rome was devastated by a terrible plague and amongst its first victims was Pope Pelagius. With churches left empty, under an avalanche of fears, sadness and deaths, the people of Rome turned to a young deacon as their new bishop. This was Pope Gregory. Himself keen on medicine, he understood that the "wounds of the soul" are more hidden than the "wounds of the body". What the sick people of his city were in desperate need of was a "remedy", a "cure", an "immunity" – yes; but a spiritual, as well as a medical one. What was needed in the sixth century and is still needed today are *medici cordis*

– physicians of the heart – men and women who can see, name and heal the deeper, and often hidden, spiritual wounds of Covid and post-Covid. With the help of these men and women the Church becomes "prophetic", that is, able to go beyond descriptive new words.

The Psalmist denounces the consequences of a lack of this prophetic ministry, when saying: "let their eyes be blinded so they cannot see, and their backs be bent down for ever" (Psalm 69 (68):24). Pope Gregory explains that the "eyes" are those who by reason of their calling have received the office of guiding from on high; but if they lack vision, those who are attached to them and follow them – who are called "backs" – will suffer the consequences. Where "eyes" lack vision, where the Church is not prophetic, the "backs" of humanity are weighed down under the burden of fears and darkness.[1]

In this small booklet, I will turn to different "eyes": to eyes that remained open in the midst of terrible sufferings and illnesses; to the eyes of a pastor for his afflicted sheep; to the eyes of sentinels who whilst in the dark have "not sinned against the light";[2] to weak and sick eyes, still able to read souls and guide them; to the inner eyes of discernment; to eyes whose wisdom has been purified by suffering; and to

---

[1]   St Gregory the Great, *The Pastoral Rule*, I.

[2]   St John Henry Newman, *Apologia pro Vita Sua*.

merciful eyes. I will borrow the eyes of Thérèse of Lisieux and Charles Borromeo, John Henry Newman and Ignatius of Loyola, the Abbé Huvelin, Job and the Virgin Mary. They can teach us how to be a prophetic Church in a time of Covid and post-Covid so that our "backs" may not remain bowed down for ever, but instead, spiritually renewed and interiorly transformed, we can guide our brothers and sisters.

Father Ivano

fr. Ivano.

"Son of Man, what do you see?"

Before bringing forth words, a prophet bears a vision: God *in* history. The office of a prophet is to discern the presence and the action of God in the often opaque and painful history of a people, and make its interpretation resound. "Son of Man, what do you see?"; with this question God formed and reared prophets, a different breed from previous seers or visionaries. This is still true today. What do you see in the midst of our time? A problem to be solved? A suffering to alleviate? A plague to be eradicated? What prophets are able to see are not the mere events surrounding a people, but their meaning and therefore a concrete way to interpret history and meet God inside of it.

Addressing his priests as Bishop of Rome, Pope Francis called them to "announce and prophesy the future, like sentinels announcing the dawn that brings a new day".[3] This "new day", our future, the so-called *New Normal* – the pope warned in his Letter – will either be something new, or it will be something much worse than before. The future of humanity is something the Lord Jesus is calling the Church, both priests and people, to build up with eyes of faith: faith in the suffering, death and resurrection of Christ. We call this the Paschal Mystery: the descent of Jesus into darkness, the underworld, his death, his rising, his victory and the gift of his life-giving Spirit. The Paschal Mystery is the only historical event which has happened, and which is still happening, whose proclamation can heal the world and change the interpretation of history. To see this event is to see the "V-shaped curve" so much longed for during the pandemic.

TEMPTATIONS AGAINST PROPHECY

Pope Francis has also warned against the many temptations typical of this time: grumbling over the difficulties we face, trying to resolve them only with substitute or palliative activities, waiting for everything to return to normal, ignoring the deep wounds around us, a paralysing nostalgia for the recent past that makes us say "nothing will ever be the same again", the imbedded logic of repetition or preservation.

---

[3]   Pope Francis, *Letter to the Priests of the Diocese of Rome*, 31st May 2020.

All these temptations can be encapsulated in the attitude of the third servant of the well-known Parable of the Talents in Chapter 25 of Matthew. A man gives to each of his three servants talents – extremely valuable ancient coins – before going away for some time. In the Greek text the word used for "time" is *chronos*, that is, our history, our present day, the pandemic, our hopes and sufferings. The man in the story is not a money-lender, nor a sower or a reaper; he is the Lord of time, he represents Jesus. Throughout the whole Gospel of Matthew, Jesus has a second name, Emmanuel – "God-is-with-us" (*Mt* 1:23). The talents in the parable are "of God", their value given by the very presence of God in them. It is true that all the servants, all of us, are living in a time where the face of God, his voice and his presence have been taken away from us, but we still have his coins, his talents.

The tradition of the Church, from early on, has associated the talents with the Word of God, the events, the facts of our life, through which God speaks to us. These events, these talents – we know from the parable – carry the capacity to bring fruit, the power to generate new events, new life. One event we have all received is of course the present pandemic.

To produce more talents is to enter into this event and see its full meaning; to bury the talent is instead to dissociate oneself from the event. While still recognising that there is something in it which is "of God" – that is, God is calling us to engage with it, open a dialogue with it, trade with it – the third servant of the parable does not enter the event

ΝΥΞ

ΗϹΑΙΑϹ

ὄρθρος

he has received. And so, that event buried underground remains sterile, its meaning does not appear, the new does not come from the old, and the servant is left in darkness and suffering. In the parable there is a unique expression, not used elsewhere in the New Testament and the Greek version of the Bible, "the joy of the Lord" (*Mt* 25:21,23). Those servants who trade their talents and produce more, experience this joy. By entering into the events of our life – including the pandemic – at a deeper level, beyond their literal sense, our life can take on a new meaning.

In Christian art there is a beautiful image which describes the office of a prophet. Represented, in this miniature from the tenth century *Paris Psalter*, as standing between the Greek personifications of Night (νύξ) and of Dawn (ὄρθρος), the prophet separates them, and makes the transition from one to the other happen. With eyes raised to heaven, the prophet "sees" the hand of God, the action of God *in* history.

The transition between the night of this pandemic and the dawn of a new day is not so much a chronological one, Covid and post-Covid – no; it has to do with whether or not we are able to discern the presence of God and his action in the present. This is why we need prophets, to help us to decipher God's calligraphy in our history and so lead us out of darkness into a "new day", and not a post-Covid day only.

CHAPTER ONE

The Eyes of Thérèse

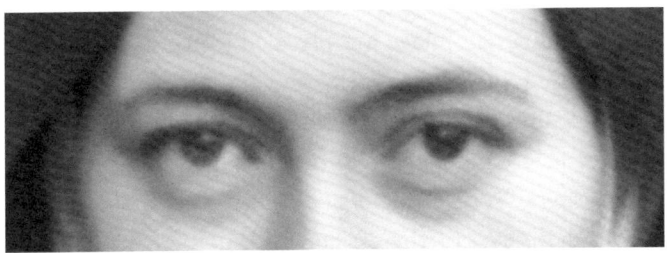

THÉRÈSE AUX ROSES

When Céline Martin, a keen amateur photographer and an art student, entered the Carmel in Lisieux in 1894, she took with her a small 13cm x 18cm black box; it was her camera. Nineteenth-century France was then a pioneer in the newly developing industry of photography. Céline, Sœur Geneviève de la Sainte-Face, would capture her young sister Thérèse posing inside the cloister. With her artist's eye and intimate knowledge of her sister's soul, she retouched the photographs in her cell. Her floral and cosmetic additions were not meant as embellishments, but rather to bring to light Thérèse's true appearance.

For more than seventy years, Céline's Thérèse, typified by the image of the saint holding a crucifix covered with roses – Thérèse *aux roses* – was to be the only authentic authorised representation of Thérèse of Lisieux. Eight months after Céline's death early in 1959, the Carmel began preparations to publish all the existing photographs of Thérèse in their original, unvarnished form. When the photographs were released in 1961, under the title of *Visage de Thérèse de Lisieux,* a different image was revealed which did not match the sanitised "doe-eyes" type. A much more complex figure replaced the chubby-faced fifteen year-old novice, the intelligent-looking eight year-old and the religious posing on a carpet of roses. A diversity of true faces appeared, and above all, the eyes of Thérèse appeared in their truthfulness, revealing the journey of her soul.[4]

A photograph is you at a particular moment; you cannot hide, it captures your soul. Thérèse aged three and a half, the beautiful open dove-like eyes of a child, with nothing to hide, an innocent gaze. Then the tragedy of the death of her mother, so great a shock for a very sensitive and touchy child that she was unable to recover for ten years. A long emotional crisis, difficulties at school, spiritual trials, constant scruples, physical illnesses, grieving for a series of separations: everything became a cause of suffering for this sad adolescent. Eyes half-closed, hidden, reveal a broken

---

[4]   François de Sainte-Marie, *Visage de Thérèse de Lisieux*, Vols 1-2, (Lisieux, 1961).

spirit, eyelids half-way down, an incredible amount of pain in her eyes.

THÉRÈSE AUX TÉNÈBRES

> God permitted my soul to be invaded by the thickest darkness…this trial was to last not a few days or a few weeks, it was not to be extinguished until the hour set by God himself… I would like to be able to express what I feel, but alas I believe this is not possible. One would have to travel through this dark tunnel to understand its darkness.[5]

The word *ténèbres* (deep thick darkness) appears eight times in the last part of her autobiography, yet it made its first appearance in its early pages, as Thérèse recounted the trial she lived on the vigil of her religious profession and the anguish which entered her soul.

> The beautiful day of my wedding finally arrived. It was without a single cloud; however, the preceding evening a storm arose within my soul the like of which I had never seen before. Not a single doubt concerning my vocation had ever entered my mind until then, and it evidently was necessary that I experience this trial. In the evening, while making the Way of the Cross after Matins, my vocation appeared to me as a *dream,* a chimaera… I found life in the Carmel to be very beautiful, but the

---

[5]   St Thérèse of Lisieux, *The Story of a Soul*, Manuscript C, 5v°.

devil inspired me with the *certainty* that it was not for me and that I was misleading my Superiors by advancing on this way to which I was not called. The darkens was so great that I could see and understand one thing only: I did not have a *vocation*.[6]

The eyes of Thérèse had to enter even deeper darkness before opening again. "Suddenly" – she writes six years later – "the fog that surrounds me becomes more dense, it penetrates my soul and envelops it in such a way that it is impossible to discover within it the sweet image of my (heavenly) country; everything had disappeared!" To make herself even better understood she makes darkness speak:

Tired by the darkness all around me, when I want to find rest for my soul with the memory of the luminous country I aspire for, my torment redoubles. Darkness itself seems to borrow the voice of sinners, mocking me saying: it is all a dream, the light is a dream, this talk of a heavenly country, of a God who made it all, who is to be your possession in eternity is a dream. You think one day you will come out from this fog which surrounds you. All right, go on longing for death! But death will not give you what you hope for; it will only mean a night darker than ever, the night of mere non-existence (*la nuit du néant*)![7]

After these words, a long full stop.

---

6   St Thérèse of Lisieux, *The Story of a Soul*, Manuscript A, 76r°.

7   Ibid., Manuscript C, 6v° [author's own translation].

THE NIGHT OF MERE NON-EXISTENCE

In what is perhaps the most striking passage in her autobiography, *The Story of a Soul,* Thérèse of Lisieux, writing to her prioress Mother Marie de Gonzague, spoke, not without some hesitation, of the "quality" of the darkness which oppressed her spirit during the last eighteen months of her life. Our own darkness too has a quality, a certain colour and intensity which is not out there external to me, but it is lived out in me, not without strong physical and emotional pain. Her *nuit du néant* can help those of us who have looked into our spiritual depths and are tempted to flee. Thérèse *aux roses* unfortunately could not do the job. What is described here is an unprecedented spiritual struggle where darkness is not a vague emotional blockage or an abstract questioning, but it is a real existential presence. Hans Urs von Balthasar describes Thérèse's experience as a suspension between earth and heaven, like the cross, physically and spiritually, hanging in the void with the Lord with no attachment to either earth or heaven.

Writing of the *nuit du néant,* Thérèse was not playing with words or using a rhetorical pious expression, so familiar to her Carmelite mystical spirituality; no, she was speaking from *within*. She was not preaching a spiritual retreat to novices; she had really entered into darkness, in fact, she had plunged into the abyss, a sheer fall. She underwent its full power and experienced its chilling force, where negation became eternal and her memory became nothing more than a further deepening of what was not. She wanted to uncover more of herself, but said, "I am afraid I may have said already too much..." She had entered the abyss of her soul, and she was somehow aware that she could not traverse this thick darkness with the aid of the maps already available to her in the Carmel, and known to her prioress; she had to go beyond the confines of what she knew. But we need to be careful not to project a nice *happy end* to her experience and to any experience of darkness.[8] Somehow, from the outside Thérèse knew all of this and she willed this, but from within it was a completely different story. This was a completely new world where not only had her loving God disappeared, but it was a world ruled by powers and fears she had never experienced before.

The period from May to September 1897 was for Thérèse one prolonged process of dying. As her physical body was dying, her spirit was facing death too. What for any other person takes place quietly and privately without witnesses, for Thérèse happened as if under a clinical microscope. When we read the *Last Conversations,* the dialogues of the bedridden Thérèse in the infirmary of the Carmel of Lisieux,

---

[8] To describe the existential experience of Thérèse I have drawn on Ida Friederike Görres, *The Hidden Face*, (Ignatius, 2003); Noel Dermot O'Donoghue, "The Experience of Jonas" in *Heaven in Ordinarie: Prayer as Transcendence*, (T&T Clark International, 1996); Guy Gaucher, *The Passion of Thérèse of Lisieux*, (Saint Paul Publications, 1989); Jean-François Six, *Light of the Night: The Last Eighteen Months of the Life of St Therese of Lisieux*, (University of Notre Dame Press, 1998).

we see how uncomfortable it would have been to sit next to her. "I sigh and whimper and cry out continually: O my God, my God, I cannot go on, have mercy, have mercy on me." Even her valiant sisters were shaken and frightened by the spiritual and physical attacks Thérèse was undergoing. Darkness had a clear target, and this is true for us too, to obscure her mission. As her consciousness of approaching annihilation advanced, we read more intense statements about her mission after her death: "As long as you are in chains you cannot fulfil your mission; later, after your death, will come the time of your conquests."

THE PASCHAL EXPERIENCE

It was about five o'clock on 30th September 1897, a heavy rainy day, when Thérèse of Lisieux entered her final agony. She looked pale and disfigured from her suffering and anguish. Gripping the crucifix in her hands, she appeared to surrender herself entirely to God. Her breathing became weaker and more laboured. Her face was bathed in a cold sweat, and her clothes, pillows, and even the blankets were soaked with it. She was shaking. Here are the words of her sister Pauline, Mother Agnès, who alone was by her side for most of the afternoon:

> we thought that was the end, when, suddenly, she raised her eyes, eyes that were full of life and shining with an indescribable happiness surpassing all her hopes. Sister Marie of the Eucharist approached with a candle to

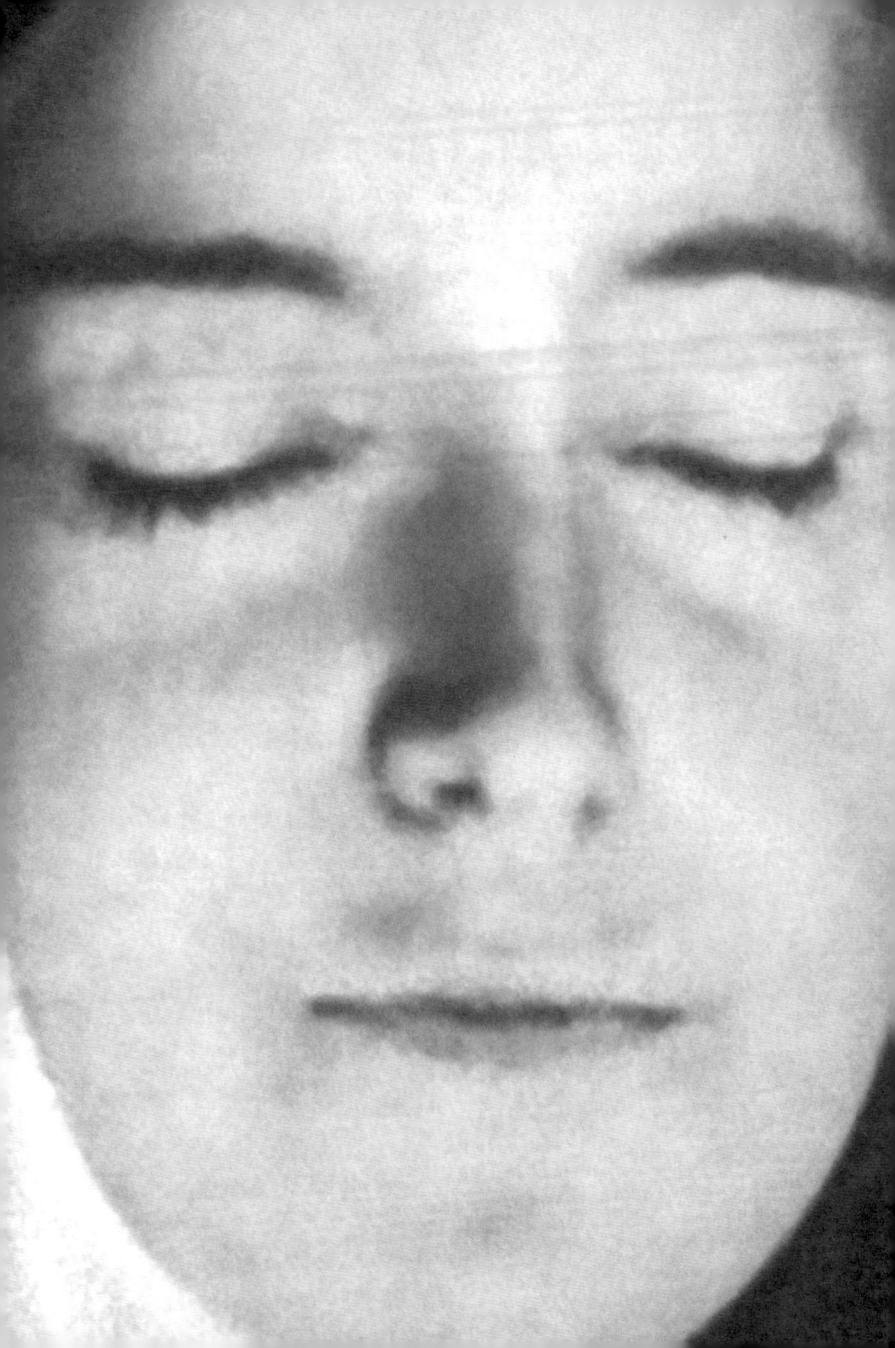

get a better look at that sublime gaze…the light from the candle passed back and forth in front of her eyes did not cause any movement in her eyelids…then she closed her eyes and the whiteness of her face, which had become more accentuated during the ecstasy, returned to normal. She appeared ravishingly beautiful and had a heavenly smile. We did not have to close her eyes, for she had closed them herself after the vision. Her face had a childlike expression, she did not seem any more than twelve years old.

"I have often tried to analyse this moment of ecstasy since then," testified her other sister, Céline, at the Apostolic Process of 1910, "to understand what it meant, for it was not only a look of beatitude; it also revealed great surprise and, in her expression, a noble confidence." The dove-like eyes of the child had finally come back.

All the accounts given by witnesses agree on what happened in the infirmary of Lisieux on 30th September 1897. The emaciated face of Thérèse changed, regaining her former glowing colour and beauty, and she looked up at the statue of the Virgin Mary in her room in a kind of ecstasy that lasted the space of a Creed, a look of great joy, strange majesty and dignity, before finally closing her eyes at seven o'clock in the evening.[9]

---

[9]   Cf. Guy Gaucher, Appendix IV in *The Passion of Thérèse of Lisieux*, (Saint Paul Publications, 1989).

The present pandemic has removed from our own images and self-images the cosmetic and floral artworks so dear to Céline Martin and revealed something we would have rather preferred to hide, the eyes of our soul and in them the spirits of fear and thick darkness. Father Bernard Bro has written of the "democratisation" of Thérèse's experience. The victory over darkness, the triumph over anguish and fear, every fear, fear of the future, fear of our own limitations, fear of others, fear of self, fear of death, fear of loneliness in the face of the future, this victory belongs to Christ and to Christians. The eyes of Thérèse and her final smile speak of a Christian experience. Those eyes and that smile exist in each one of us. In 1973, on the centenary of St Thérèse's birth, a Vietnamese priest wrote: "The mountain people here, the primitive peoples, are haunted by fear, fear of spirits. To dare, as Thérèse did, to smile at a spirit? To say *Our Father* to a spirit? To dedicate oneself to loving a spirit? What a revolution!"[10]

---

[10] Bernard Bro OP, *Saint Thérèse of Lisieux*, (Ignatius, 1996).

CHAPTER TWO

Sheep Dogs and Hunting Dogs

HAVE MERCY, O HOLY CRUCIFIX!

On Sunday 15th March 2020, six weeks into Italy's lockdown, Pope Francis went on pilgrimage through the streets of his city, Rome. Yet there are plenty of chapels along the naves of the papal Basilica of St Peter's and many holy grottoes in the Vatican gardens. When Pope Francis left the Vatican walls that Sunday afternoon it was not for some outdoor exercise or to recite some prayers; no, he was heading for a very specific place. Walking for about half a mile on foot, the pope entered the Church of San Marcello in Via del Corso and stood there before a large dark wooden crucifix, praying for an end to the pandemic. This same crucifix the pope wanted next to him on the evening of Friday 27th March 2020 when, from a deserted St Peter's colonnade, he invoked the mercy of God upon the city of Rome and the whole of humanity.

In 1522, as a violent plague struck the city of Rome, this same crucifix was carried in a penitential procession from the Church of San Marcello to St Peter's Basilica. Fearing the risk of contagion, the civil authorities tried to prevent this happening, but Roman nobles, clerics, barefoot youths with heads covered in ashes, and citizens in black habits, carried the wooden crucifix through the streets of the city crying "Have mercy, o holy crucifix!" The chronicles of the time report that the procession lasted from the 4th to the 20th August. Sixteen long days, to cover a distance of half a mile! As the crucifix proceeded the plague receded, so each *rione* of Rome tried to hold on to the sacred image for as long as possible. When the crucifix returned to the Church of San Marcello, the plague had completely ceased. Fifty years later, another shepherd, also barefoot and with a crucifix in his hand, went on pilgrimage through the streets of his own city, calling for mercy for his flock afflicted by the plague.[11]

SAN CARLO AL LAZZARETTO

On 11th August 1576, the plague erupted within the city walls of Milan. Initial rumours soon turned into spreading

---

[11] John Peter Giussano, *The Life of Saint Charles Borromeo*, (Burns and Oates, 1884).

fears. All those who could – senators, nobles and wealthy merchants, the Governor of the city as well as the Grand Chancellor – left town and took refuge in their castles in the countryside. As horses and carriages were hastily leaving a terrified city, Charles Borromeo, Archbishop of Milan, who had been out of city for the burial of a bishop friend, heard of the outbreak and at once mounted his mule and turned back to Milan. He dismounted at the Duomo and after a short prayer rode to the northern quarter of the city, where the plague had started, to visit the sick and the dying. On his return to his residence, he found those local civil officials who had the courage to stay. They were completely lost, their leaders gone, and begged the archbishop to take charge. Conscious of the risks, Borromeo prepared for death by making his will and putting his affairs in order; he shaved his beard as a sign of sadness and penance, and began ministering to the material and spiritual needs of his plague-stricken flock.

In the north-east district of the city, between Porta Venezia and the central railway station, stands today the small octagonal Church of San Carlo al Lazzaretto. The Church was built on the site of a big leper-house, a large quadrangular columned cloister with almost three hundred rooms where the sick infected by leprosy and plague were confined. In the middle stood a little chapel, built above the ancient temple of Santa Maria della Sanità (Mary, Health of the Sick), open on all sides so that the celebrant could be seen by all the sick patients in the cells of the *lazzaretto*. The building was surrounded by a moat full of water like a fortress, and was only accessible by the gate. Every day Borromeo went to visit the sick and when the building became overflowing with plague victims and the gate was barred, the archbishop walked around its perimeter praying as the lamenting inmates begged for a blessing.

To shelter the sick, Borromeo bought six large plots of land outside and around the town walls, and built wooden and straw huts. When supplies ran out, he begged for money (especially at Rome from generous cardinals), organised special collections across his own diocese, sold his own personal possessions including the gold and silver ornaments of his private chapel, and even tore down curtains from the Bishop's Palace to use them as fabric to care for the sick in the lazarette houses. Appealing to his priests, he said:

> We have only one life and we should spend it for Jesus Christ and for souls, not as we wish, but at the time and in the way God wishes. It would show great presumption and neglect of our duty and God's service to fail to do this, with the excuse that God could not replace us by others more capable of working for his glory. This does not mean you should neglect human means, such as preventatives, remedies, doctors, everything you can use to keep off infection, for such means are in no way opposed to our doing our duty. God can replace us!

When many of his brother bishops, including the pope, begged him not to put his life at danger and urged him to use all possible caution, Borromeo answered: "From the beginning, I resolved to place myself entirely in God's hands, without however despising ordinary remedies…a sponge soaked in vinegar and a few aromatic herbs in the mouth!"

CARING FOR BODY AND SOUL

The only paternal authority left in the city, Borromeo gathered a scientific commission of professors and practitioners advising him on how best to keep the infection at bay. A "plague directory" was published, and republished in 1630 when yet another plague struck Milan. He urged the Milanese to carry out corporal works of mercy, wrote and distributed a small booklet as a spiritual insurance policy for those left with no access to the sacraments, and gave permission to the clergy to administer the sacraments under all conditions. Special indulgences were granted. It became normal to see priests baptising, hearing confessions and giving holy communion in the streets of Milan. Borromeo himself administered the sacraments to the afflicted and when he found doors barred, he was seen entering infected huts through the windows by making use of a ladder! Still, he would take all the necessary stringent hygiene precautions. For himself, he acted as if he was actually infected, allowing no one to come near him, keeping (in his days) to a "rule of eight" in his household. Walking in the city, he made sure

that "social distancing" was kept: he was accompanied by a servant waving a stick to make sure no one would get close to touch his robe or beg for a blessing. He would give alms only by placing coins in jars of vinegar, he often changed his vestments, sanitised everything with vinegar and fire, and carried with him a sponge soaked with vinegar and herbs which was regarded as disinfectant. How familiar all of this is!

Taking advantage of a brief alleviation in the contagion, Borromeo led three large penitential processions from the Duomo, with rules for "social distancing". All began as on Ash Wednesday with blessed ashes put on their heads, calling them to penance and conversion to newness of life. Borromeo walked barefoot through the city with a rope around his neck, like a condemned criminal, carrying a crucifix in his hand (still preserved this day in the sacristy of the Duomo), singing "have mercy on us, have mercy on us". Some of his contemporaries accused him of encouraging the spread of the pestilence by assembling people in processions and public prayers. In fact, the processions dispersed fear and encouraged the faith of the Milanese that the pestilence, by the grace of God, would finally come to an end.

"O REVEREND FATHERS"

As the pestilence reached the level of calamity, the city was cut off from the outside world, and turned into a huge *lazzaretto*. Deserted streets, all commerce halted, empty churches, thousands dependent upon alms, and the city finances on their knees. Throughout all of this Borromeo continued to give alms, feed the hungry, and care for the souls of his people. Borromeo called for priests to minister to the spiritual needs of the afflicted:

I have no need to describe to you the miserable state of the city…yet, this I will say, that it is no ordinary calamity which we have to endure…we see men in the hour of need deprived of the presence and support of those nearest and dearest to them. This would be grievous indeed if it only concerned the frail bodies which must one day perish…but here it is worse than this: it is not their bodies alone which are in danger of perishing, it is their souls, for which I plead… O reverend fathers, here is your opportunity…to you we look, who ought to be ready to lay down your lives for the love of God and your neighbour, especially when it is a question of saving souls… Though we have spoken of the duty of not counting our lives dear to us in his cause, we do not wish you to understand that there is of necessity danger to health or life, by God's grace it is far otherwise, and with ordinary caution and attention to rules, risk may be avoided. But this we say, that if it should please Almighty God that any of us should catch the infection and die, that it would be a glorious end, rather deserving the name of life, for dying thus in the service of God and of our neighbours, it is most certain that we should attain to life eternal… Shall we suffer ourselves to be overcome by the fear of death?… Fear not, my brethren, I myself shall keep my eyes upon you and will never forsake you. For my own part, you are my witnesses, that from this hour I devote myself to minister to you in holy things. I am firmly resolved that no weariness, no fatigue, no peril, shall make me quail from fulfilling any pastoral office, of doing everything in my power for the souls which God has committed to my keeping.

The zeal of Charles Borromeo for souls and his love was even more contagious than the disease itself! At his plea many priests offered themselves and were straightaway appointed to their tasks, and every day more priests joined them. From that day onwards there was never to be any lack of priests during the whole time of the plague.

At the same time, Borromeo understood the need to minister to those in quarantine whose time in isolation could have opened the door to idleness and temptations to sin. For this reason, he made provisions for "spiritual seeds" to be spread across the city. Seven times a day and seven times each night, church bells would ring inviting the people to pray for the end to the plague. At the sound of bells, the Milanese would go to their windows and a priest would lead them in prayer, while, on their knees, they sang their responses following a prayer book printed by the archbishop. Nineteen stone columns with a cross at the top were erected across the city and were visible from most houses. Altars were also erected at crossroads, where priests would celebrate daily Mass, so that those in quarantine could participate from the windows of their homes. Confessors went from house to house, sitting on the doorsteps whilst the penitent knelt inside. Parish priests went around with the Blessed Sacrament on Sundays, and gave holy communion on the doorsteps to all. To help the people in their spiritual fight, the archbishop sent around a pastoral letter on how to spend time in mental prayer and a list of spiritual reading.

THE MERCY OF GOD ALONE

The number of new cases in Milan started to diminish by Christmas 1577, and by January 1578 the plague had disappeared at last. It was calculated that around 17,000 had died in the city itself and 8,000 in the surrounding countryside, and only 120 priests among them.

What should be done once a pandemic has passed? In the Hebrew Bible there is no word for "history"; rather, the word used is *zachor*, which means "memory". This is quite different, because it means to see the hand of God at work in history and to be able to read his handwriting. As the pestilence left, Borromeo published a small booklet for his beloved people entitled *Memoriale* – "A Remembrance". In it, he wrote:

There is one thing, my children, of which we must make mention, which will make us appreciate more fully the magnitude of the mercies we have received at the hand of God. Have always before you this great benefit which God has so miraculously worked for you, and never be at any time unmindful of his mercy.

In a sermon during the Mass of thanksgiving with all the clergy for the end of the plague, speaking of the deliverance from the pestilence, Borromeo said:

This is not by our prudence, which indeed failed us at the very outset, and left us bewildered and lost; nor is it due to the skill of physicians, who have not yet discovered so much as the origin of this malady, much less the means of counteracting it; nor does it come of tender care for the sick, for they were at the first outbreak deserted by their nearest and dearest. No, my children, no; let us never fail to acknowledge this – it was the effect of the mercy of God alone.

In January 1584, Charles Borromeo gathered together, for the last time, all the parish priests of the city of Milan. Perhaps reflecting once again on the experience of the plague, he presented to them a meditation on the shepherds of Bethlehem as figures of the parish priest as shepherd of souls: "There were shepherds…who were keeping watch over their flocks by night" (*Lk* 2:8). The eyes of a shepherd are called to remain open during the night, when thick darkness comes down, pointing out to others the way, and when the evil wolf attacks, they are called to defend the flock and not run away like hired men (cf. *Jn* 10). And yet, warned Borromeo, often the shepherds "are all dumb dogs, they cannot bark; dreaming, lying down, loving to slumber" (*Is* 56:10). Comparing the pastoral care of souls to a kind of hunting, with priests and bishops as hunting dogs, Borromeo spoke of two sorts of dogs used for hunting: those sent into the forest to scare the wild animals and make them come out into the open, and those sent after the fleeing animals to run them down.

We too, priests and bishops of Covid and thereafter, are to meditate upon to the words spoken by the plague's bishop, St Charles Borromeo. We need to have open eyes and a hunting nose. We are shepherds, it is true, called to defend and nourish the sheep afflicted by the wounds of the pandemic and its consequences, but we are hunting dogs too, called to smell out the scent of spiritual dangers and temptations, to name the fears oppressing our people and help deliver them. This is what allows us to discern between prophets and spectators, between good shepherds and hired men.

LITANY OF ST CHARLES BORROMEO

(to pray in time of anxiety and fear)

Lord, have mercy.	*Lord, have mercy.*
Christ, have mercy.	*Christ, have mercy.*
Lord, have mercy.	*Lord, have mercy.*
Christ, hear us.	*Christ, graciously hear us.*

God the Father of heaven, *have mercy on us.*
God the Son, redeemer of the world…
God the Holy Spirit…
God the Holy Trinity One God…

Holy Mary, *pray for us.*
Holy Mother of God…
Holy Virgin of virgins…

St Charles, imitator of Christ *pray for us.*
St Charles, faithful follower
   of Christ crucified…
St Charles, replenished with
   the spirit of the apostles…
St Charles, consumed with zeal
   for the glory of God…
St Charles, Father and Guide
   of the Clergy…

St Charles, the light and support
of the Church…
St Charles, a model of humility
and penance…
St Charles, most desirous of
the salvation of souls…
St Charles, most zealous for
the instruction of youth…
St Charles, ardent in prayer during
the great plague…
St Charles, full of love for those
afflicted by the great plague…

Pray for us, O glorious St Charles,
that we may be made worthy of the promises of Christ.

Preserve your Church, Almighty God, under the protection of St Charles Borromeo. As he was eminent in pastoral love for those afflicted by the plague, so may we learn how to love and pray in this time of anxiety and fear. We ask this through Our Lord Jesus Christ your Son, who lives and reigns with you in the unity of the Holy Spirit, one God for ever and ever. Amen.

CHAPTER THREE

No 6 Rue de Laborde

With a pandemic, as with most traumas and unexpected tragedies, our external world shrinks and becomes uncertain and unsafe. Despite our natural desire for control and protection, no boundaries are safe enough and we end up retreating into our mind and thoughts. For many the step towards depression and mental illness is not very large. I know of a man, psychologically deeply scarred, far from being mentally and emotionally balanced, full of fears, whose eyes were able to read and to write in the very souls of people; a holy man far from being whole himself. The inner eyes of the Abbé Henri Marie-Joseph Huvelin are perhaps more needed today (and tomorrow) than ever before.

THE LIGHT AND THE SOLACE OF SOULS

Without exaggeration, he is one of the greatest, and least known, spiritual guides of the nineteenth century. Widely read in Greek, Latin and French classics and modern literature as well, he was able to talk about any newly-published book and quote from any of the Church Fathers. A former pupil of the prestigious École *Normale Supérieure,* professor emeritus of the *Petite Seminaire*, the Cardinal Archbishop of Paris had his eyes on him for the chair of Church History at the newly-established *Institut Catholique.* "Why did he decline the offer?" asked the Rector of the *Institut* at the Requiem Mass for the Abbé celebrated in 1912: "Because he wished to give himself absolutely to the care of souls, because that mission, for which God has endowed him with supernatural gifts, was to him the highest that a priest could undertake." In the words of Baron Friedrich von Hügel, who spent more than twenty-five years under his guidance, Abbé Henri Marie-Joseph Huvelin was:

a distinguished Hellenist, a man of exquisitely piercing and humorous mind, he could have become a great editor and interpreter of Greek philosophical or Patristic texts, or a remarkable Church historian, but he had chosen instead to *"write in the souls of people"* whilst occupying, during thirty-five years, the unpaid post of *vicaire auxiliare* in a large Parisian parish. There, suffering from gout in the eyes and brain, and usually lying prone in a darkened room, he served souls with the supreme authority of self-oblivious love, and brought light and purity of heart to countless troubled, sorrowing or sinful souls.[12]

A PRIEST BETROTHED TO HIS PARISH

Born on 7th October 1838 – the Feast of Our Lady of the Rosary – his teenage years at the lycée are marked by a litany of academic prizes; honours in arithmetic, French and Latin language, geography, history, grammar. In the midst of his studies he kept alive his interior life where the question of his vocation remained open. He passed all his exams with distinction, and, despite his father's strong opposition, entered the seminary of the French College in Rome. Ordained a priest in 1867 for the Diocese of Paris, he was appointed priest-attached to the well-off parish of Saint-Eugène. "His first parish", he used to say, "is for a priest the betrothed that God bestows on him." The parish newsletter mentioned thirteen Sunday Masses, from six

---

[12] Michael de la Bedoyère, *The Life of Baron Friedrich von Hügel*, (J.M. Dent & Sons Ltd, 1951).

o'clock in the morning to one o'clock in the afternoon. There were plenty of good reasons for the newly appointed *vicaire* to remain unobserved, and yet "when M. Huvelin preached, one could see that he believed what he said", commented a young parishioner in her dairy. Again, "the preacher sent everybody to sleep…but not the Abbé Huvelin! The Gospel as he explained it had become real and alive." He was able to touch the heart and his Sunday sermons became more and more frequent and well attended.

In 1875 Huvelin was transferred to the newly-built large parish of Saint Augustin, in the bourgeoise Parisian VIII *arrondissement*. In this church, not the most beautiful in Paris, he remained as a simple curate until the day of his death. Very soon the crypt with its capacity of six hundred seats became too small for all those who wanted to attend his "little lectures" and catechism classes, and the queue outside his confessional became so long that a side chapel of the church had to be used as a waiting room. Families even moved the time of their Sunday roast in order to be present at his regular Mass. Well prepared beforehand, his homilies and lectures were somehow improvised as they were delivered. "When I am talking" the Abbé confessed "I have too many ideas, so they jostle each other; they are like excited fishes, trying to get out…but my throat is too narrow for them!" One of those present at his regular one o'clock Sunday Mass has left us a memory of him:

His face was flushed and a little swollen, there was nothing impressive about his appearance. He might even have seemed rather ordinary…but when he started speaking! Expressing himself with perfect ease, in language stripped of all ornaments, he used to comment on the Gospel, at once reaching the highest spirituality, yet making it easy of approach and practical. Very bent, leaning sometimes on the edge of the pulpit, he was clearly having some physical suffering…his sufferings made the man; he walked with his head leaning rather to the left, like a man who had been crucified.

A FATHER TO MANY

When not at the pulpit or in the confessional, our curate spent his day at No 6 rue de Laborde, around the corner from the church. Here, the "Apostle of Paris", as the newspapers began referring to him, received flocks of people during the day and answered their letters at night. His clientele included bohemian misfits and fashionable intellectuals, Sorbonne professors, aristocrats living in the chic boulevards Malesherbes and Haussmann as well as their working-class servants, Parisian ballerinas and enclosed Carmelite nuns. All felt themselves at home with him. In one of the obituaries which appeared after his death in 1910 we read:

On 10th July there passed away a figure whom veneration and even legend had already surrounded with something of a halo…the radiance of that mind and that soul was truly extraordinary and his influence, which was silent and hidden, but deep and lasting, can only be compared with that of the saints.

Apart from the celebrated converts – one amongst many, the Viscount (now Saint) Charles de Foucauld – there was a wide twilight zone where dwelt lost and wondering souls of all kinds.

What brought so many people to No 6 rue de Laborde? The Abbé was not a one-size-fits-all *convertisseur*. He believed too much in the mystery of the Incarnation and knew that each soul was unique and demanded unique attention and patience. Above all, love guided him and all felt the charity of a guide who first of all poured out on them love, gave them the time and space to restore their broken hearts, and helped them to stand firm till they could walk by themselves.

For thirty-two years, in the isolation of his study and his confessional, on his bed of sickness, he gave light, he revived, he restored, he made peace and he converted. He could help and advise in connection with all the ills of the soul. From the far ends of France there came to him the broken-hearted, those distressed in conscience and those whose spirits were wavering; they went home satisfied with the unique answers that they had awaited, which were just what they needed and seemed to have been thought out and provided for each individual and for that special occasion.

Yet this eminent and sought-for director of souls, familiar with Plato and translator of John Chrysostom's *On Priesthood*, a mystic according to many, was a far from healthy priest; in fact, quite the opposite. He was an invalid who gave light. The Abbé Huvelin ministered whilst in a permanent state of chronic and debilitating ill-health. Those who came to see him regularly exchanged medical bulletins about his health. Far from being an obstacle to his ministry, his illness seemed to be the source of his light.

At rue de Laborde, the Abbé used to receive visitors in the afternoon. On entering his study, on the first floor, they would come into a rather small room full of books, papers, letters and stray sheets of paper piled up everywhere. On the wall, near the window, a small picture of St Francis of Assisi, and above his bed the wooden crucifix left to him by his uncle, Dom Eugène Huvelin, a Cistercian monk who died in the odour of sanctity. Often in a darkened room because of bad migraines, the Abbé always dressed in his soutane, sitting in a velvet English-style armchair, with a cat on his crippled knees, perhaps lessening the acute pain of the rheumatism that affected him. When his black cat Blanchette died, he gently refused the offer of a new one, saying, "One does not love twice!" Marie-Louise, Huvelin's faithful housekeeper, used to accompany visitors from the tiny ante-room to the study. Huvelin was a true reader of souls; meetings with him would not last too long. There was no beating around the bush; instead, he went straight to the point, and the point was the soul of the visitor, to which the Abbé spoke prophetic words. Many visitors remarked how very few words were necessary, the Abbé somehow "knew" and his answers came quickly with luminous precision. In the mornings the house-keeper often found out that his bed had not been used. It was not rare for him to spend the night on the floor, praying, with his arms in the form of a cross.[13]

This "physician of souls" was himself overwhelmed with illnesses of all kinds, both physical and psychological. Within his frail and deformed body lay a not dissimilarly frail and broken spirit. In one of his notebooks eleven pages were found covered with his signature and the chilling sentence *Il n'est* – "he does not exist!" It should not come as a shock to know that this man endowed with spiritual discernment and enlightenment suffered from acute depression and suicidal feelings. The Abbé Huvelin was a man deeply wounded by lack of self-worth, emotional fears, mentally and psychologically unbalanced. A man far from being whole, whom we can even dare to call mentally disordered. And yet, this invalid and diminished priest, unable to leave

---

[13] For the life of the Abbé Huvelin I have drawn from Charles Chauvin, *Petite Vie de l'abbé Huvelin*, (DDB, 2008); *Charles de Foucauld, Abbé Huvelin, 20 Ans de Correspondence entre Charles de Foucauld et son Directeur Spirituel: 1890-1910* (Nouvelle Cité, 2010); M-Th. Louis Lefebvre, *Un Prêtre, L'Abbé Huvelin*, (P. Lethielleux, 1968).

his armchair, scarred by past fears and negative thoughts, troubled in body and mind, had prophetic words for many, many souls and gave light to blind souls.

One day, one poor woman who wanted to meet the Abbé, in trying to make herself understood, referred to him as "the priest who has a miraculous illness". "He had a gift", wrote one of the regular visitors of No 6 rue de Laborde, "difficult to define…that of fully understanding someone who had up to then been quite unknown to him…and of seeing their inmost heart".

There is no vaccine against the deep-seated fears this pandemic has brought to the surface. For many, inner darkness, self-doubt, conscious and unconscious fears are a real spiritual "long Covid". Many souls need to find their way to No 6 rue de Laborde!

CHAPTER FOUR

The Cannonball which Transforms Souls

WHIT MONDAY 1521

In May 1521, an army of twelve thousand men gathered together to attack the citadel of Pamplona. Within the unfinished fortifications of the town were only a thousand weary soldiers with a handful of artillery pieces. The commander was ready to surrender, but Iñigo was not. Conscious of the hour, he made his confession to one of his fellow soldiers, with whom he had fought many battles and who knew his sins, then took his place on the ramparts of the citadel. After six hours of heavy bombardment there came the cannonball which changed his life: "a cannon shot hit his leg and broke it, and because the shot reached the inner side of the one leg it damaged the other as well." The garrison surrendered; it was Whit Monday 1521.[14]

The Frenchmen looked after him with courtesy, doing all they could to treat his broken leg. His wounds were too severe to be treated there, so the invalid was carried on a stretcher through the Navarre heights for a two week journey until he reached his native Loyola. Here his sister-in-law prepared the best room in the family castle. His was a desperate case. To avoid his right leg remaining crooked it had to be broken again and set straight; and so it was. Iñigo chose to bear the excruciating operation with no anaesthetic. It all seemed in vain though as fever set in and his condition worsened. Death was at the door, and the last sacraments were administered.

On the eve of Saints Peter and Paul, our dying man received a grace. At midnight, his health started to improve, but it was not over yet; as the bone of his leg began to heal, a protrusion made his right leg shorter than the left. This was the end of his military hopes and dreams! Unless…he could undergo a new surgical operation to cut the bone and forcibly lengthen his leg. Iñigo was ready and endured once again the terrible pain. Forced to remain still in his bed for months, his eyes stared at the oak beams of the roof in his

---

[14] John Olin, *The Autobiography of Saint Ignatius of Loyola*, (Harper & Row, 1974).

sick-room. Not quite prophetic eyes! Yet the cannonball which crushed his body was about to transform his soul. We know him as St Ignatius of Loyola.

BETTER OR WORSE?

Speaking about the pandemic, Pope Francis, companion of St Ignatius, has said: "We are experiencing a crisis. The pandemic has put all of us in crisis. But let us remember… after a crisis a person does not come out the same. We either come out of it *better*, or we come out of it *worse*". This was true for Ignatius of Loyola in 1521 and it is true for us today. A sudden stop sign, weeks of forced lockdown, and even the attic room of a castle feels like a prison cell. Time, time, plenty of time to think, and so old passions, past sins stored inside oneself come to the surface. Anxious, bored, with plenty of time on his hands, our house-bound patient asked for those romantic knight-errant stories he loved so much, but none of them were to be found. Instead, his pious sister-in-law – we all have a guardian angel! – took from the library four leather-bound volumes written by a Carthusian monk on the life of Christ, and a thick book, a collection of the lives of saints. As Ignatius read them, page after page, he became fond of them and, putting his reading aside, began to think about the things he had read. He read of how his alter ego in Assisi became the most transparent image of Christ; he read of Dominic scourging himself in the night for his own sins and the sins of others; and of the monk Onofrius and the battle against the devil fought in the desert. So Ignatius pondered over the choices made by these saints. How much influence these three saints' stories had upon his future life!

These thoughts lasted a while, but when other matters intervened, worldly thoughts returned and he spent much time on them too. And so, in the mind of Ignatius, God and the world linked together. What had started as a time of convalescence, necessary to heal his leg, turned into a deeper healing experience. Thinking and pondering, contrasting thoughts and images became entangled as one and the other alternated. Stuck in hesitation and confusion, Ignatius made a discovery which allowed his whole experience to shift:

> There was this difference. When he was thinking about the things of the world, he took much delight in them, but afterwards, when he was tired and put them aside, he found that he was dry and discontented. But when he thought of going to Jerusalem, barefoot and eating nothing but herbs and undergoing all the other rigours that he saw the saints endure, not only was he consoled when he had these thoughts, but even after putting them aside, he remained content and happy.

HIS EYES WERE OPENED A LITTLE

His experiences of God and the world appeared to be similar; both lasted a long time, both were engaging. Yet a difference between them made him feel *better* or *worse*; his feelings, during and after, were of happiness or of sadness. In the attic room of Loyola castle, the eyes of a prophet were being formed, gradually and painfully:

> One day his eyes were opened a little and he began to marvel at the difference and reflect on it, realising from experience, that some thoughts left him sad and others happy. Little by little, he came to recognise the difference between the spirits that agitated him, one from the devil, the other from God.

"Hurry, come down, for I must stay at your house today" (*Lk* 19:5). Meditating on these words which Jesus spoke to Zacchaeus, a young nineteenth-century French Carmelite wrote: "What is this descent that he demands of us except an entering more deeply into our interior abyss? This is not an 'external separation from external things', but a 'solitude of spirit', a detachment from all that is not God."

Ignatius of Loyola – whose name means "fire" or "burnt by fire" – would have understood very well the spiritual experience lived by Elisabeth of the Trinity:

> As long as our will has fancies foreign to divine union, whims that are now yes, now no, we are like children; we do not advance with giant steps in love, for fire has not yet burnt up all the alloy, the gold is not pure; we are still seeking ourselves; God has not consumed all hostility to him. But when the boiling cauldron has consumed every imperfect love, every imperfect sorrow, every imperfect

fear, then love is perfect and the golden ring of our alliance is larger than heaven and earth. This is the secret cellar in which love places his elect, this love leads us by ways and paths known to him alone; and he leads us with no turning back, for we will not retrace our steps.[15]

TRANSFORMATION OF SOUL AND DELIVERANCE

On his bed sick, in lockdown, Ignatius was undergoing a deep spiritual journey: from thoughts to the awareness of them, from pondering to focused reflection, from learning from one's experience to understanding it, from seeing the movements of one's heart to the discernment of the spirits. Little by little, this man turned into being a prophet of his own heart, able to recognise what was God's work and what was not. "A transformation of soul": this is how Ignatius described these long weeks in Loyola. What followed after – the solitude of the Charterhouse of Miraflores near Burgos, the night time vigil of prayer and repentance for his past sins at the feet of the dark Madonna of Montserrat, the mystical school in the cave at Manresa with its "spiritual exercises" – was but a journey of deliverance from those evil spirits he had learnt to discern and name in the castle of Loyola. The cannonball was continuing to have its long-lasting healing effects.

---

[15] St Elisabeth of the Trinity, *Heaven in Faith, Second Day*.

Can you name *your* cannonball? Can you point at that sudden event which has broken something in you, something in us, our habits and securities, our plans and ideas? That cannonball is not pure tragedy; no. Ignatius never cursed Whit Monday 1521! As his eyes opened, little by little, to see the hand of God *in* his history, our eyes too can be opened to see, within the "cannonball" of our pandemic, the movements of our heart and discern what inside of us is born from God and what is not. Spiritual and mystical experiences are not lived out inside a clean holy laboratory. It was a forced painful long lockdown which transformed the soul of Ignatius and made of him a prophet of the spirits. Let us not curse *our* own cannonball.

A PRIVATE LITANY OF HUMILITY

From the desire of being praised,
   deliver me, Jesus.
From the desire of being honoured…
From the desire of being preferred…
From the desire of being consulted…
From the desire of being approved…
From the desire of comfort and ease…
From the fear of being humiliated…
From the fear of being criticised…
From the fear of being passed over…
From the fear of being forgotten…
From the fear of being lonely…
From the fear of being hurt…
From the fear of suffering…

That others may be loved more than I,
   Jesus, grant me the grace to desire it.
That others may be chosen and I set aside…
That others may be praised and I unnoticed…
That others may be preferred to me in everything…
That others may become holier than I,
provided I may become as holy as I should…

O Jesus, meek and humble of heart,
   make my heart like yours.
O Jesus, meek and humble of heart,
   strengthen me with your Spirit.
O Jesus, meek and humble of heart,
   teach me your ways.

O Jesus, meek and humble of heart, help me put
my self importance aside to learn the kind of
co-operation with others that makes possible the
presence of your Father's household.

Adapted from a prayer by Rafael Cardinal Merry del Val
from *The Prayer Book for Jesuits.*

CHAPTER FIVE

A Strange Providence

Coronavirus diaries have become a popular means of expressing moods and capturing in words or even emojis unique personal experiences.

If I am in sickness, my sickness may serve him, in perplexity, my perplexity may serve him. If I am in sorrow, my sorrow may serve him. He does nothing in vain. He knows what he is about. He may take away my friends. He may throw me among strangers. He may make me feel desolate, make my spirits sink, hide my future from me. Still, he knows what he is about.[16]

---

[16] St John Henry Newman, *Meditations and Devotions.*

When John Henry Newman wrote in his diary of "sickness" and "perplexity", "sorrow" and a "desolate spirit", he was referring to three concrete experiences of his life, including an epidemic which brought him very close to death. "[God's] Providence" – wrote Newman – "is in fact not general merely, but is, on the contrary, particular and personal."[17]

CONVERSIONS

When Newman was fifteen, his middle-class family went through a very difficult time. His father, a banker in the City, had to change jobs following the failure of his business. Consequently, the family had to move house; the young Newman found, during the long summer holiday of 1816, a time for reading, reflection and solitude, made more intense by an illness and convalescence. This clever teenager, set on a trajectory which was making him more and more intellectually self-sufficient and sceptical about religious truths, experienced his "first conversion". "A great change of thought",[18] as Newman put it in his autobiography, it went far beyond the intellectual sphere and left a lasting and deep effect in his spiritual life. Newman found himself confronted with the realisation of the sovereign presence of a personal God in his life, a presence – "myself and my creator" – he was trying to avoid. Years later, in his letters, Newman would several times go back to the experience

---

[17]   St John Henry Newman, *Essays Critical and Historical*, II.
[18]   St John Henry Newman, *Apologia Pro Vita Sua*.

of 1816, recognising it as providential: "the heavy hand of God came down heavy upon me"[19] and his "wonderful grace turned me right round".[20]

A "second conversion", also bound up with an illness, occurred in 1827: "the heaviest affliction with which the good hand of God has ever visited me".[21] As a young tutor at Oriel College, Oxford, Newman overdid it. Too much reading and intense work, mental fatigue and stress brought about a kind of nervous breakdown. The proud and intelligent young don found himself in a state of exhaustion, confused, unable to think and recollect, unfit to speak in public. Added to this was the sudden death of his beloved sister Mary. Illness and bereavement did their providential work in the man. Forced to spend a long time in solitude convalescing, Newman was granted eyes to see how imbedded in him were intellectual pride, self-reliance and vainglory. Once again illness was a providential moment used by God to readjust Newman's religious course.[22]

MY SICILIAN ILLNESS

A "third conversion" and illness happened during a trip to Sicily in 1833. In his mid-thirties, together with some sympathetic friends, Newman set sail for a Mediterranean tour: Christmas and the New Year in Malta and the Greek

---

[19] St John Henry Newman, *Autobiographical Writings.*
[20] St John Henry Newman, *Parochial and Plain Sermons*, I.
[21] St John Henry Newman, *Autobiographical Writings.*
[22] St John Henry Newman, *Apologia Pro Vita Sua.*

islands, then Palermo, Naples and finally Rome. Here, Newman decided to leave the group and go back to Sicily alone. "From that time, everything went wrong" he explained. At Leonforte, in the heart of Sicily, he caught a fever that had become a rampant epidemic in the island and in many cases proved fatal. For a week, Newman had persistent constipation and haemorrhoids, suffered from high temperature and a wearisome constant cough. He especially dreaded the long nights spent in delirium and hallucinations; as he laid sleepless and restless on his bed, he was haunted by his past sins and found himself in the midst of an intense spiritual struggle.

Once again, illness, loneliness and physical weakness became "the weapons of heaven's grace"; their fruit, the eyes of a prophet who could say, "at last I knew *why*". Newman could see how "it was his self-will" that God had been "attacking". His illness had brought to the surface his deep-seated sin under the form of attachment to his own self-will. His Sicilian illness was about more than self-knowledge. Newman was granted the grace to name and renounce the very sin which was an obstacle to the mission God had in view for him once he was back in England. When, a few years later, Newman reflected on this experience, in the midst of still confused memories, there was something he could see very clearly: "I shall not be able to recollect everything in due order...I seem to see, and I saw, a strange providence in it." In a note of 1840 added to the account of his Sicilian illness, Newman asked himself: "what am I writing it for? Whom have I, whom can I have, who would take interest in it?" Meticulous details were not important, nor was self-reflection and the rationalisation of the events; what was important to him was to "see" the (strange) hand of God *in* it. This is why in the letters to his mother written in 1839 from Lyon, announcing his imminent return, Newman completely passed over the particulars of the story – "my further adventures when we meet, please God, by word of mouth" – to convey its deep meaning: "Wherever I am, God is God and I am I".

ONE MORE DIMENSION

Two years after his return from Sicily, Newman considered it necessary to raise a "red flag" about the consequences of bodily suffering. Putting it bluntly, physical suffering, in itself, can actually make us worse! "Let it be well understood," said Newman from the pulpit, "that it has no sanctifying influence in itself...pain does not commonly improve us, but without care it has a strong tendency to do our souls harm". "Weak health," clarified Newman, "instead of opening the heart, often makes a man supremely careful of his bodily ease and well-being...querulous, self-willed, fastidious, and egoistical". Pain and fear can easily lead to self-absorption as they "individualise us in our minds, fix our thoughts on ourselves, and make us selfish."[23] Newman's perception

---

[23] St John Henry Newman, *Parochial Sermons*, III.

echoes Pope Francis, who at his Wednesday Audiences has repeatedly warned us against the possibility of coming out from the pandemic crisis worse, much worse than before.[24]

How is it, then, that "when Newman came back out of Sicily, he came like a man reborn, with all his powers released and with such exuberant confidence and energy that his friends at Oxford actually failed to recognise him; all his doubts and hesitation were left behind. The shy and sensitive young don had become a leader of men"?[25] In his book on Newman's life and spirituality, Louis Bouyer points to something instinctive in Newman which dates back to his childhood and had stayed alive in his consciousness, one of the permanent truths of his life: "the world in which we live is infinitely vaster than we take it to be. It is far deeper than we are wont to imagine, and it has one more dimension over and above those we are accustomed to assign to it."[26]

Everything that took place in Newman's trip to Sicily, the circumstances leading up to his illness as well as the illness itself, can be entirely explained from a natural perspective, yet it is through this "one more dimension" that Newman experienced his Sicilian illness (and all his illnesses) and

---

[24] Cf. Pope Francis, General Audiences on "Healing the World", in particular those of 19th August, 26th August, 2nd September, 9th September 2020.

[25] Christopher Dawson, *The Spirit of the Oxford Movement*, (Sheed and Ward, 1945).

[26] Louis Bouyer, *Newman: His Life and Spirituality*, (Ignatius Press, 2011).

came out of it a "new man". The same is true for us. All that we have been through, our worldwide illness, can all be explained and even solved, yet without this "one more dimension", without this "strange providence", we remain caught up in the phenomena, the details and the particulars, and we remain orphans of the light.

CHAPTER SIX

Fear and the Gift of Sight

TASTE AND AFTERTASTE

Fear. If we could condense the time of pandemic into a taste, it would taste of fear. Even when all of this has left us, we could all still find ourselves with its aftertaste, like a spiritual "long Covid". Is it possible instead to come out from our trials with a gift? Yes, a gift! Can we find ourselves in a new place, a step ahead of where we were before all the sufferings we have been through? There is a man in the Bible, his name is Job, who went through deep and sudden suffering in body and psyche; he found himself afflicted, misunderstood, accused; he lamented with words and in silence, and still came out from all his trials with a *gift*, the gift of a prophetic sight.

This man is "a son of the East", not an Israelite, and as such Job represents every man. Job is me and you, his experience of human vulnerability is ours: "my life is like a breath"; "like a flower, such a one blossoms and withers, fleeting as a shadow, transient"; "on earth it passes like a shadow", "made of clay…back into dust". When suffering knocks at Job's door, it is a "reality check" in his relationship with God. This is true for us too when suffering comes to visit our families and friends, or our own lives. In his commentary on the Book – the *Moralia in Job* – Pope Gregory the Great describes this moment of truth as a moment of revelation, when the life of a virtuous and deeply religious man turns into the life of a prophet:

> This man [Job] endowed with all the virtues, was known only to himself and God. Without his sufferings, we would not know him at all. Just as the odour of perfume cannot be carried far unless it is blown about, and as the smell of incense only grows strong when it is burnt, so we know only such virtues of the saints as can be known through their trials.[27]

FEARER OF WHOM?

From the start of the Book, the narrator describes Job as someone who "fears God". Throughout the narrative, the innocent suffering of Job works to dismantle the traditional

---

[27] St Gregory the Great, *Moralia in Job*, I.6.

understanding of "the fear of the Lord", according to which those who fear God prosper, whilst the impious are afflicted by trials and sufferings. Job's fear of God is put under question by Satan and by his friends; from the suffering of a just man arise a crescendo of anguished questions. In all of this, Job never doubts the existence of God, but precisely because he believes God is responsible for everything that happens in the world, he wants to know why it is that God has now chosen to remain hidden and refuses to intervene.[28]

God's answer does not sound like an answer at all. God asks Job how good he is at hurling lightning, making the sun rise and set, producing the rain, setting limits to the waves of the sea. In a cascade of images taken from sea and sky, from the earth and the underworld, God reveals to Job his power. It sounds like a provocation, but it is not. God chooses to communicate with Job through the lens of creation, in order to expand his vision of reality. With this cosmic lens, Job begins to see creation and history with new eyes, the eyes of God. It is true that Job already knew of the cosmic power of God, but from a human perspective. What Job knew was a God who dominates and a man who is dominated; a divine capricious God misusing his unfathomable power, whose wisdom cannot be comprehended. Such knowledge and fear of God are of no help to Job in the midst of his sufferings,

[28] For a reading of the Book of Job, I have drawn from the works of Robert Alter, *The Art of Biblical Poetry*, (Basic Books, 2011); Gianfranco Ravasi, *Giobbe*, (Borla, 2005).

and are not helpful to us either in the midst of our own sufferings. A deeper knowledge of God, not from a text-book but shaped by suffering, has to appear; a *gift* greater than Job's virtue and deep religious nature.

A NEW FEAR AND A NEW VISION

The answer of God is a sort of diastolic movement responding to the systolic movement of Job's lamentations. As Job shuts down one by one all the dimensions of creation including the very womb that gave him birth, God responds by expanding all the dimensions of creation, opening up one by one all the elements of the cosmos, all things of nature, all the animal world. Everything from God's perspective is ruled by a logic of expansion; everything is interpreted through images of generation of life. Where Job yearns for darkness, God affirms light; while Job invokes an eternal night without the stars of morning or of twilight, God recalls the first moments of creation when the morning stars sang together with the children of God.

The man known as a fearer of God has to learn to fear God in a new way, proper to his new existential reality. The most significant expression of this new fear concerns the sea and its mythological monsters, biblical images of our deepest terrors. Job knew of a mighty God who tramples the waves of the sea, but it is only from the challenging voice of God that Job learns to fear God not on account of his conquering power, but because of his fatherly care. As a father sets laws and limits to his children, so God sets limits to the waters of the sea and bolts doors against the chaotic impetus of its waves. As God brings order out of chaos in nature, so will he do in Job's life. Doors are closed so that the tide of death cannot overwhelm the land of the living: "thus far shall you come, and no farther, and here shall your proud waves be stayed"; and again, "I shut in the sea with doors when it bursts out from the womb". The wisdom and love of God for his creation, in setting boundaries to the primordial deadly sea, is now what constitutes Job's fear of God.

"NOW MY EYES SEE YOU"

In the midst of his lamentations, Job recalls his conception and the moment of his birth, wanting to go back to his mother's womb and shut himself in there for ever. In a spiral of pain, he prays for deep darkness, longing for eyes that would never again see the opening of dawn. His eyes, blinded by suffering, are unable to see the providential work of God; yet the Book ends with Job's eyes seeing something new. This is why Job is a sign of hope for us all. If, at first, Job simply confesses his inadequacy in understanding God's work and desires to remain silent, he afterwards admits his arrogance and having obscured the designs of God concerning the things he did not understand. From the heart of the existential storm where Job finds himself, the gift of new sight is granted to him; Job's suffering has acted as a time of gestation for prophetic eyes which are finally able to see God *in* history: "I had heard of you by the hearing of the ear, but *now* my eyes see you."

On the eve of All Saints 2020, from his Covid hospital bed following days in intensive care, Cardinal Gualtiero Bassetti, President of the Italian Episcopal Conference, decided to write an open letter on the holy Eucharist. A strange place and a strange moment, we might say, to share theological thoughts on the Eucharist. We all know – don't we? – the importance of the Eucharist in our Christian life, but suffering can give us a new knowledge, an experiential knowledge; a given truth can become even more true for us. When Cardinal Bassetti calls for the Eucharist not to be left on the margins of our lives, but put back, with even greater force, at the centre of our life; when he refers to the Eucharist as the soul of the world and the fulcrum on which the whole universe turns, we hear the voice of Job "fearer of God" after his trials, we hear of a new sight of God, we hear of a *gift* which could only be born *now*, out of suffering.

CHAPTER SEVEN

Mater Misericordiae, Pray for us

On 20th June 2020, the Feast of the Immaculate Heart of Mary, in the middle of the global pandemic, Pope Francis added three new invocations to what we familiarly call the Litany of Loreto, a list of invocations of titles of the Virgin Mary followed by the request "pray for us" which is often recited at the end of the Rosary. These additions are not pious extras or Marian devotional whims, quite the contrary; they have in themselves a prophetic nature. "Referring to the present times, marked by feelings of uncertainty and trepidation," states the Letter from the Congregation on the Divine Liturgy which approved the new invocations, "the People of God devoutly have recourse to the Virgin

Mary, full of affection and trust." Prayer has a prophetic character. It is a response to how we interpret the events that surround us.

One of the three new Marian invocations is *Mater misericordiae* – "Mother of Mercy". There are many artistic representations of Mary with this title. One I only discovered recently when visiting the Diocesan Museum of Bressanone. It is a part of a larger panel, which looks like a diptych, showing the mysteries of Christ and Mary side by side. At the bottom right is a familiar yet unusual image of Mary as Mother of Mercy. What was familiar was her gesture of spreading wide open her mantle, creating a place of refuge and protection for the whole of humanity. What was unusual, at least to me, and which caught my attention, was that her mantle is in fact a shield against arrows being shot down from the quiver of God the Father!

I have since discovered that the image of the arrows and the protective mantle of the Virgin Mary are indeed part of a traditional iconography called *imagines contra pestem* (religious images against the plague). In Central Italy especially, there are many examples of medieval processional banners – *gonfaloni della peste* – which depict the Mother of Mercy in her role of stopping adversities and afflictions with her salvific mantle-shield.[29]

---

[29] Louis Reau, "Iconographie de l'art Chrétienne", Tome Second, *Iconographie de la Vierge*, (Presses Universitaires de France, 1957) pp. 116-117.

What about the image of God shooting arrows, then? Does is it mean that God has sent a plague-arrow to us? To speak of God's wrath is not in fashion at the moment, and we do not like to think of a God who is angry. And yet it is part of the fatherly role to correct, to admonish and to chasten; it is part of the charism of being a father. What about the image of Mary, what is her charism? She is not simply standing there as a passive shield, no. With eyes turned to God, she is actively engaged in a prayerful relationship with the Father, interceding for us and in this way giving birth to mercy. In prayer the eyes of Mary become prophetic eyes, able to see a merciful Father. If you look once again at the painting, you notice that most of the arrows are broken whilst still in the hands of God the Father.

A variant of the image of Mary breaking the plague-arrows can help us to expand our vision. In other paintings of the same theme, the arrows are not directed at men and women, but aimed at the personification of their sins. The arrows, seven in number, represent the seven deadly sins, our sins, each one of them fatally pierced by an arrow.

Our Lady of "plague-broken arrows", *Mater misericordiae,* it is under your mantle that we can now see; we can see our sins, and we can see the Merciful Father.

Sub tuum praesidium confugimus,
Sancta Dei Genetrix
Nostras deprecationes ne despicias
in necessitatibus
sed a periculis cunctis libera nos semper,
Virgo gloriosa et benedicta

Beneath your loving mercy,
God's Mother, we take refuge.
Do not despise our prayers.
In all our needs please help us,
and in all dangers save us,
O glorious and blessed Virgin.

IMAGE CREDITS

Cover image and page 17: *St Thérèse of Lisieux* © Office Central de Lisieux.

Page 6: Roman Catholic Church of Saint Peter and Saint Paul, Clerkenwell, London.

Pages 11 and 14: *Prophet Isaiah with the Night and the Dawn*, Folio 435v *Paris Psalter,* Bibliothèque Nationale de France.

Page 24: *St Thérèse of Lisieux* © Office Central de Lisieux.

Page 27: *Crucifix of San Marcello*, Church of San Marcello al Corso, Rome, Italy.

Page 32: *St Charles Borromeo*, (engraving) by G. Edelinck after Charles Le Brun. Wellcome Collection.

Page 41: Abbé Henri Marie-Joseph Huvelin (1838-1910), priest of the Church of Saint Augustin, Paris.

Page 51: *St Ignatius of Loyola* (engraving) by Lucas Vorsterman I (1595-1675). The Elisha Whittelsey Collection, The Elisha Whittelsey Fund, 1951.

Page 61: *St John Henry Newman* by Lady Coleridge (née Seymore), 1876. © Mazur/catholicnews.org.uk.

Pages 69 and 72: *Job in Despair* by Marc Chagall, lithograph printed in colours, 1960. Photograph courtesy of Sotheby's, 2021.

Pages 77 and 79: *Intercession: Mary's mantle of protection* (c.1515) attributed to Vigil Raber. Diocesan Museum of Bressanone, Italy © Hofburg Bressanone Bressanone.

Seeing the Pandemic with Eyes of Faith

Seven Prophets for Our Time

Fr Ivano Millico

All booklets are published
thanks to the generosity of the supporters
of the Catholic Truth Society

ISBN 978 1 78469 654 2